reginald stowe

sunsets in

Harlem

sunsets in harlem

reginald stowe

IBSN: 9798612819554

sunsets in harlem

3

to all the people who were told their vulnerability is a weakness.

sunsets in harlem

sunsets in harlem

by reginald stowe

sunsets in harlem

within your hands is my story:

a reminder
to open your hearts
believe in yourself
that the pain you feel
is only temporary
and to never stop choosing
love.

sunsets in harlem

table of contents

-

sunsets in harlem

it was gentle morning in harlem
when a child asked me
why i loved the sun so much.
as my skin began to glow
i say.
the sun tells me
it is okay to leave
when things begin to end.
but most importantly
it is how you come back.
and share your light
with everyone around you.

— intro

sunsets in harlem

i hold

on to

the hurt.

sunsets in harlem

reginald stowe

they ask to wear our skin
because it is beautiful.
we ask to have their privilege
only to turn bitter
with pure disgust
because
all lives matter.
i do not understand.
you have taken our wings
weakened our voices
and yet you still demand
we fly just like the rest
of the flock.

— double standards

sunsets in harlem

we sit in a unified circle as children.
going one by one asking our dreams as adults
i am asked
what do you want to be when you grow up?
the other children say the typical answer
doctor
nurse
policeman
my voice shakes and hands glisten
as if my words were an animal desperate for
freedom
with fog dripping from my lips like
overcast skies on a cold bitter day.
i say
i want to be a man with blue eyes
blonde hair
a little pale skin
and maybe even bigger ears
so that my mother can never fear
her son's life being stolen from him.
so that her son
may never be seen as a walking target
but a living and breathing human.

reginald stowe

i was taught at a young age
that my life was no longer in my control.
but at the hands of a society that picks and
chooses
what we can and cannot be.
i had to learn
to be comfortable with death.
after seeing many other brown boys on the
news
again
again
and again.

— the day i learned about racism

my father
was the first
man to teach me that
being left behind
was the expectation.

— father

reginald stowe

when the world stopped moving
and you were
not there to hold me.
a thousand words brewed inside me.
yet none of them can explain
how hard it was to watch you
be happy.
to not be in your life
and a wife by your side.
i still get texts from your mother
asking if i'm doing alright
i tell her i am fine
but we both know i am lying.
you see
i knew what i wanted to tell her
but how selfish would it be
to bring back washed up memories
when i am supposed to be teaching myself
to live without you in this morbid reality.
so i keep these jumbled words
that not even twenty-six letters can form
and think to myself
they say when you love someone
you cannot describe it.

but i wonder if sadness counts too.

reginald stowe

he asked me
'have you ever been in love'
i say no.
but my heart whispers
'yes. but not the kind that stays'

i am not sure
if i can ever talk about love.
without your name
spilling from my lips.

wearing voices all day is exhausting

— codeswitching

sunsets in harlem

i was a clumsy magic trick
performed by a foolish magician
that i did not figure out
until everything was over.
blinded by the affection
of this one-sided love.
two-sided desire.
disguised by the belief
that his mixture
of laughter and intoxicative smile
was the epitome of a love that
could not be divided by
the color of my skin.
to his friends
i was the rabbit he pulled out his hat.
the soul he sawed in half.
and like that
he disappeared.
with no reason at all.
tricked to believe
it was worth something.
i was worth something.
and i was wrong
again.

reginald stowe

i miss the summer
when the heat of the sun makes the pavement
burn the soles of my feet.
i miss the fall
when the sunlight begins to fade and and i no
longer feel the crisp cool wind.

i figured the older i've gotten that life was just
missing things in different intervals.

at my age, i miss when days were just for
burning. i miss when the only concerns i had
were being home before the streetlights came on.
or using my imagination to play knights &
dragons.

i am sure you have realized by now. i miss a lot of
things.

and today most of all,

i miss you.

— nostalgia

to fill the cup
of someone
who never craved you
to begin with.
to pour yourself
until you are empty and
believe you are full.
maybe that is why
when you left
i did not feel anything.

— empty i

i have an infatuation
with empty things.
empty cities.
empty streets.
empty houses.
empty towns.
things that shouldn't
be empty.
it is the anxiousness.
and the desire to be filled
with something
that speaks to me.
because i know
it is a feeling
that hits closer
to home than i'd ever
be willing to admit.

— empty ii

the darkness is my friend.
it seems that when we are
together.
it is the only time i can write.
when i feel it all.
and the stars begin to flow
from my heart into my hands.

— midnight

reginald stowe

some days
my words
get caught in my throat.
and all i can do
is drown in them.
it is perhaps
when i have the most
to speak
that i say the least.

— social anxiety

my silence
knows
how to scream too.

— do not underestimate me

if they call themselves
dark.
i will call myself
grey.
light nor
dark.
satisfied.
but unsatisfied
happy and sad.
all at the same time.

— inbetween

when the weight of you
was lifted.
a lot of things
became difficult
like sleeping.
talking.
breathing.
anything and
everything
suddenly became heavier
without you.

— tell me how does that work

reginald stowe

i poured so much hope
into your aching hands
and all i could do
was watch it slowly
drip through the cracks
of your fingertips.
i was the love that kept
giving even
when you gave me
nothing
in return.

— baggage i

i don't typically get jealous.
but when i see you.
i always feel jealous.
not because i want to be
someone else but
because you gave others
the same kind of attention
i needed from you.

— attention

they wrap these
words in honey
as if mixing the two
between a compliment
and an insult
will make them taste
any sweeter.

— you are not that black

you treated me like a dream.

the one you forget as soon as you
wake up in the morning.

reginald stowe

i don't know why
i am so afraid to let
something go.
even when you left
the ghost of you
still danced in the
palm of my hands.
even when you left
i was still holding
on to you.
when you never held on
to begin with.

— baggage ii

your lips
have so much beauty
yet so much torture.
i made the mistake
of hanging onto your every word
and ended up killing myself.

— noose

reginald stowe

i was wrong
to expect you to
love me
and replace the pain
for not
loving myself.

— reflection

maybe one day
i will look upon
the stars as i think of you.
but deep inside.
i know.
somewhere.
you'll be there.
thinking of her instead.

i built a fence around my heart
to keep you out.
and it was just as destructive
as the one i once built
to keep you in.

— fortress

i have never felt lonelier
than laying in the arms
of someone i know
won't stay.

— needy

you hold against me
how i acted while
you were
taking every single
part of me.
i never knew i could say
things like that.
but then again
i did not know you could
either.

— verbal

sunsets in harlem

untouched i lay here
as i fall down another staircase
into my thoughts.
wandering further and further from myself.
when you drifted away
i could not tell the difference anymore
since you were another boy left once more.
but this time.
i loved you.
and while i had many words i wanted to say.
they bit my tongue like razors
baring all the pain of broken silence
with thoughts just as violent.
digging deeper.
and deeper into my self-esteem.
with degrees of anxiety reminding me
i am just another one of his fatalities.
untouched i lie here again.
untouched is the man i loved.
walking away with my blood on his hands
free from the crime that *he* committed.
acquitted of the love
i dreamt would set me free.

i ache at every thought of you

i try not to like
too many things
because when
i like it
i will begin to love it
and when i love it
it leaves.

right as the sun faded.
the world began to
look despaired of
color and a dark grey.

if only you knew.
that's how my life
looked without you.

— november 29th

sunsets in harlem

i hate coming home
knowing you're not there.
taking off my own clothes.
the sheets that contained your scent.
and my bed reminding me
of the memories
we had.
so i threw everything out.
and i will continue to sleep without them.
if i am sleeping without you.

reginald stowe

there are days.
where all i wish for.
is to break.
into hands.
that will hold me still.
until the next morning.
but all i am left with.
is my own.

i wish to live a life without the
fear of doors

some days.

.

i stand here.

.

in this body.

.

and don't feel at home.

i miss
the
feeling
you gave me
but
regret
the
pain you left.

— naïve

losing you
was not an easy
process
i knew
the moment the stars
vanished from your eyes
and the light left your soul
i lost you.
and like the rest of them
you slipped away from me.
farther and farther
each day
like holding sand in water
with no way
of making it stay.

— please stay

i wish you could hear
how much i think about
you.

waves of reminisce pour into the
recesses of my dark mind and isolated heart.
i have forgotten where to begin or start
when the hand of nostalgia caresses
my eyes to reimagine every moment
we shared.
i can still feel your breath on my shoulder
from the first snow in october.
i can still feel your hand.
and its warmth against my skin.
when you decided to walk away from me.
watching you leave was the first thing
next was seeing her instead of me.
after that i laid on the floor screaming to god
for your spirit to stop haunting me.
to no longer live forever
and leave this earth
for the better.

— replacement

the illusion of you
was better
than the reality of you.

reginald stowe

and though it seems
that love continues to run in the
other direction the moment i get close.
i will still chase after it.
but what if the thing i am chasing
was never mine to begin with.

— elusive

as i saw my world begin to crumble.
i ruined what we had
because i was hurting.
broke myself
so that you did not have to
and ended up losing everything
trying not to lose you.

— failed missions

i confused you for the silence
after the storm.
i should have known
i was wrong
from the destruction
that was left behind.

— the storm

please don't remember me
as the end.
i never remembered you
that way.
though, truthfully.

it would be easier to let you
go that way if i did.

— endings

reginald stowe

62

sunsets in harlem

so i may

never

forget.

sunsets in harlem

how can i heal
my own wounds
when i am still
trying to heal
my ancestors.

— questions

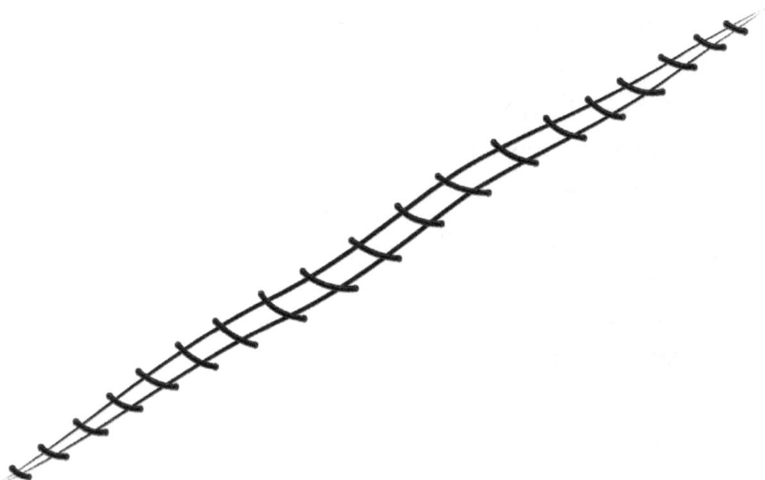

on sunny days
i talk to the flowers
asking
what it is like to be something
so kind and harmless?
to have *everything*
that keeps you grounded.
taken.
uprooted for the happiness.
of someone you don't even know.
then i realize
i am one of them too.
even while i was with you
i was wilting
in order for you to grow.
dying slowly.
every time
i was in your hands.

—— wilting

when i practice
your language
it feels foreign to me.
and it was the first one i learned.
but when
i go back to my mother tongue
it sounds like home.
smooth like
silk dancing in the river
i miss that feeling.
belonging to something.

— swahili

we do not try to stop the bad
until it happens to us.

— america

give me a minute
i told you.
deep down.
i needed more
time.
days.
months.
it was first time seeing you since you left.
and i was still trying to recover
from our past.
but.
i just missed you.
so.
damn.
much.
yes.
i should not give in to
the act of
past lovers
desperately trying
to resurrect a love
that was dead to begin with.
but drunken lips sneaked themselves
between our conversation and i told you to

hold me close for now.
and the rest will figure itself out
tomorrow.

— your sister's birthday party

reginald stowe

my cold hands
run against your body
feeling every part
as an artist does
when making his final touches.
in this rare state of mind
you gave me the possibility of love.
even if it was just for a moment
and though you are not the destination.
thank you for being the rest stop
along the way.

— the day after

when you are dealing
with an unspeakable loss
it should be time of reflection
for yourself.
and a reflection of the people
around you.

— the right ones will speak up

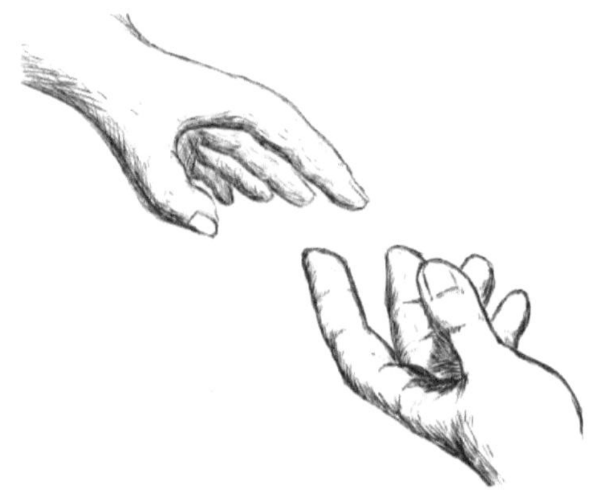

reginald stowe

forgive me
for being the worst of myself.
my doubt
is the consequence
of giving those the answers
to questions
that shouldn't have been asked
in the first place.

— me too.

i am hard to love.
that is the first confession.
but because of my complexity.
i am a rose protected by thorns.
so when you tried to touch me
and my words pricked your fingers.
you turned away.
i am more than small talk.
and fast touch.
give me conversations
on why the world exists.
give me endless possibilities
and thoughts.
if you cannot do this.
you are not ready to love me.

i am held together
by cracked lips and
soft spoken words
at 3am
on the bedroom floor.
it is what has kept me
so hopeful about finding love.
and it might be wrong.
but it has given me something
to believe in for
once in my life.

you are allowed to
uproot the foundation
in which you were grounded.
plant it somewhere else.
grow.
and you will see those starved roots
begin to harvest truth.
and the honey bees will make
a home out of you.

— toxicity

reginald stowe

i have spent my whole life
associating with one identity
that when i look in the mirror
and see another one
longing
for me to come home
i do not know what to do.
because i simply do not
know where to find it.
i am stuck in an argument
between my mother
and father tongue
and i am afraid to
say hello to both.

— mestizo

sunsets in harlem

sometimes i catch my mind
find a way to blame myself
and think
maybe if i would have
maybe if i said
as if somehow
betraying myself
would be easier
than accepting the fact
that you simply could not
understand the difference
between
yes
and no.

— victim shaming

we gazed toward each other
inch by inch.
imitating an eclipse that hasn't
happened in centuries.
your gravitational pull
brought us closer yet
i stopped.
breaking the silence.
and whispered
you are still just so far away

— immature

understand
if a man ever says
he is *not into politics*
it is simple.
he does not care enough
about himself.
his friends.
your friends.
his sisters.
mother.
grandmother.
or any living soul on this earth.
since the day we have left the womb
our existence was already political.
if that is ever his answer
that is the end of the conversation.

—— vote

just because we share the
same blood
does not mean
i am entitled to you.
if you do not deserve
respect.
i will not give it.

— kin

you told me
to give you a reason
but boy.
i am enough of a reason
myself.

if men are from mars.
then i am from the moon.
i have a damaged surface
for a soul.
dwell in the midst of the night.
and comfort those while
immersed in my own darkness.

— moonchild i

i lie awake at night
talking to the moon
because she is constantly
surrounded by darkness too.
i wonder if she feels alone
just as i do while everyone else rests.
together we fight in our most vulnerable state
and choose to share the light.
reminding others
that they are not alone either.

— moonchild ii

though as humans
we can handle pain.
it does not always mean
we should.

— black in america i

my people.
i beg you.
please.
do not become the pain
that hurt you.
do not let the hatred
they taught you
replace the love
we gave you.

— black in america ii

i would rather
take my own life.
than have mine
taken from me.

— black in america iii

sunsets in harlem

they turned us
against one another
and made us believe
that a death of our own
is the only time we must
show vulnerability.
they have rewritten all
the culture our ancestors created
and told their children that all of it
means nothing.
it is an invisible knife
that has been stabbed in our backs
for centuries.
we confuse that blood for water.
as if the bleeding will make us grow.
when in reality we are only hurting ourselves.

— black in america iiii

how can they hate us.
when their
racism.
misogyny.
homophobia.
xenophobia.
classism.
and nationalism.
are darker than my skin
could ever be.

— black in america iiiii

your nothings meant everything to me.

— appreciative

you were the love of my life
inside my head.

because of a woman.
i have learned that i
carry oceans inside of me.
because of a woman.
i am soft and hard.
light and dark.
the calm and the storm.
the flower and the thorns.
i have learned so many things
from a woman.
everything i have is because of the woman.
yet why do we treat them as if none of us
ever came from a woman.
this powerful creature.
she carries life.
and death.
those who do not see that.
should be afraid.

— a woman's work

i only have
half a heart.
but i think
my heart
has just enough space
for you.

you
may see it
as a song.
but i
hear it
as a memory.
when i ask you
to listen.
it is because
it will tell you
everything about me
that my words cannot.

— music

reginald stowe

we are the souls
our ancestors
could only dream to be
but have yet to be
the humans
we have the right
to be.

— 1865

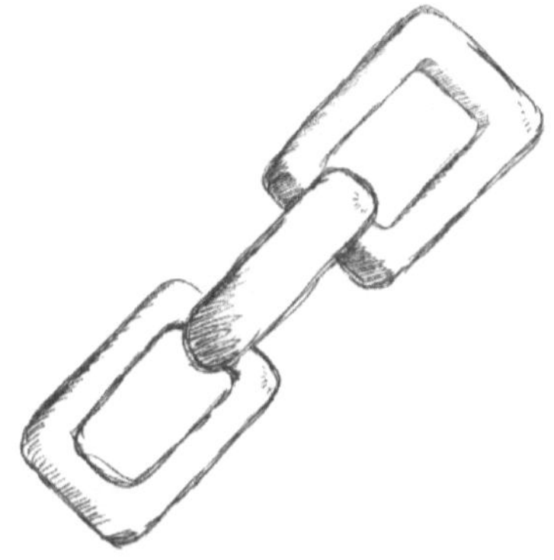

sometimes i miss the old me.
the one that was foolish enough to love.

i have an insatiable hunger to be.
be okay.
be myself.
be happy.
but at what point
will my hurting suffice
enough of my appetite
to be enough.
with skin dark and delicate
as the earth.
i am human.
fueled and pumped by love yet
made to feel
as if i don't deserve it.

— 'it's just my preference'

did you love me
just so
you can get
a quick high
from being lonely.

— my body is a drug

i had a dream
that being brown
was the norm
and being white
was the oddity.
it was strange
because
i had never seen
the world this free before.

— dreams

timelines are not linear.
others will run faster than you.
but that does not mean
you will not reach the finish line.

— take your time

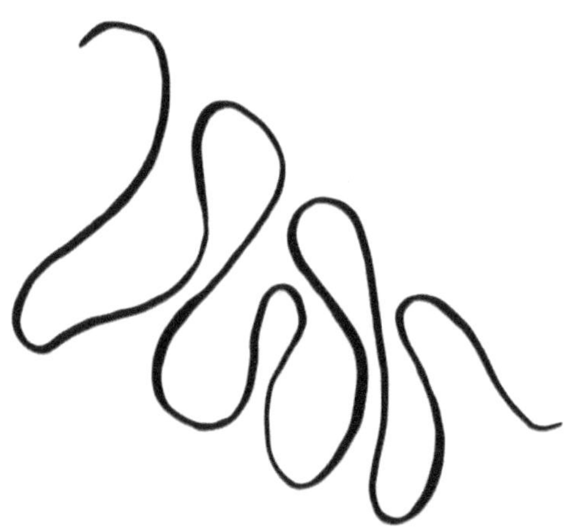

i tried to change things
by loving you harder
but i should've known
you can make love.
but you cannot make someone
love you.

— mistakes

you know me better
than anyone else.

— poetry

it has been said
there are too many of us
expressing our sadness.
too many of us
becoming poets.
i would like to start by saying
the amount of poets that are growing
is a representation of the people
our society fails to protect.
it is a symbol of the human
need for art and for anyone to deny
someone of a god-given right
will be igniting a war between
the universe that no mortal
should be exerting toward his
brothers and sisters.
secondly.
we are tired.
i am tired.
being strong all the time.
is exhausting.
and when society
victimizes.
judges.

shames us.
we will write more.
we will fight with words
that have been created
past the human imagination.
we will scream love.
pain.
heartbreak.
and we will not allow
hate to drown out our voices.
we will fight
with
every
word
until our hands bleed.
so when you say there are too many of us.
you are lying.
there will never be too many.

— we need more storytellers. we need more
vulnerability.

i got lost in the eyes of someone else
and did not search for yours.
that is progress.

sunsets in harlem

i choregraph my words
and practice what i am going to
say for hours
only to trip over my own
two feet in a failed attempt
to gracefully perform
my words for you.

— two left feet

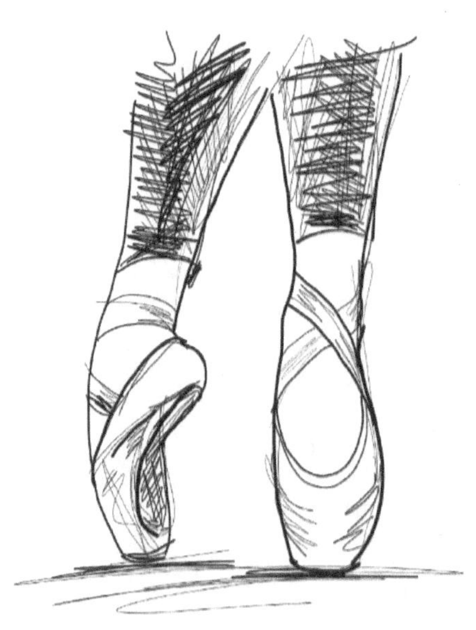

there is no right or wrong way
to handle pain
there is still
a cry in my silence
and blood in my ink.
just open your eyes.
for my unspoken words
are when my heart
truly wishes to be heard.

— unspoken words

why do i feel like
i am dying
when i am living
more than ever.

— depression

i ate the words
you told me
when you explained
why you left.
i threw them up later.
not even my stomach
could handle how fake
those excuses were.

— liar

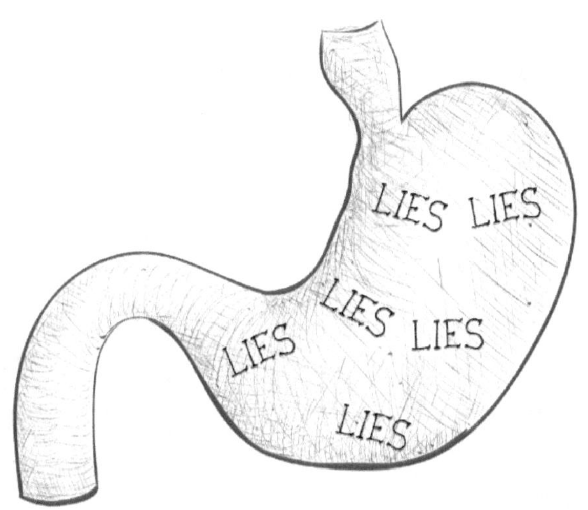

you wonder why my people
respond so aggressively to
anything and everything.
we are exhausted.
from our voices
being hidden.
and everything that makes
who we are.
ripped apart and
left with the bone
to nourish us.
we are starving.
and all we ask is
to simply exist.
in peace.
to walk down the street.
to spend time with our loved ones.
to love who we want.
and even then you
still choose to leave
us malnourished.

— aggressive

reginald stowe

i am guilted with the reasoning
of whether i should
make this story about you.
but you do not deserve to claim my happy
ending.
you were the end to a story that was never
meant to be.
gone are my days of accepting less.
not bound by your choices.
or a slave to your mind.
even when it will feel like
i won't have enough time
i will keep searching. running. dreaming.
i will run to the wildflowers
and hold conversations about how it is okay to
die and be reborn all over again.
because after all i am human.
there is too much around me
that says i should fear what's next.
so while the hills will tell me that i am small.
the mountains will interrupt and say
that everything has its place and to never worry
how small i may be to others.
that my heart will always.
always. show them what's bigger.

stubborn am i.
arms folded.
walls built.
running away just made sense.
but now.
i think i am ready to love again.
to crack open my chest.
and dig through the pieces that have
been broken.
to hand my heart over to you.
yet i warn you with caution
it is no longer what it once was
but the potential of love.
exceeds more than what it may seem
i promise.
i can love you.

— love will always win

there
was
still
truth
about
myself
hidden
in your lies.

— realizations

i tell the stars about you.
and even they shine
a bit brighter
when they hear your name.
tell me that's not magic.

— midnight chatter

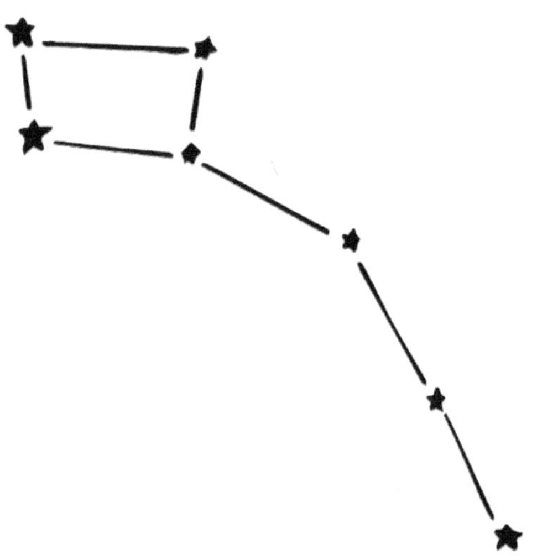

i want to go deeper with you
and make love.
not with our bodies
but our minds
with the true me.
and the true you.
take me
where no one can.
a place
where no touch can shake me.
and no kiss can break me.

— intimacy

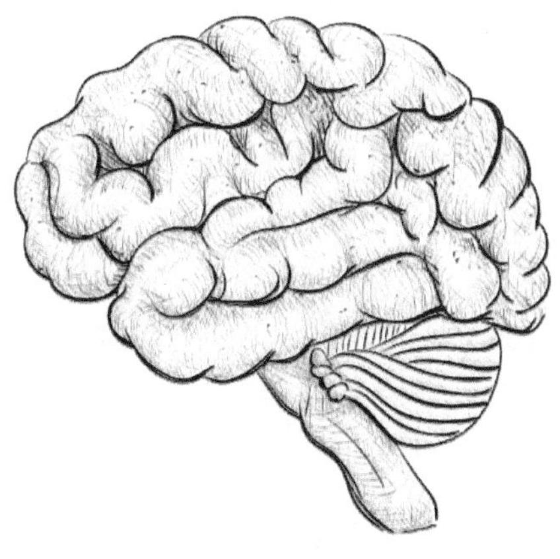

there is life.
and there is life
with you.
i want both.

— wild

reginald stowe

you ask me
what's your favorite color
i laugh.
because for a person like me
that is a question
i am hardly asked.
my own society believes
other colors
can only be complemented with
the color white.
however my love
picasso did not
create his
greatest works
with just *one color.*
without all of the colors
you miss the point of love.
love is art.
so when you asked me
what's your favorite color
i did laugh.
because i don't want just one color.
i want the whole damn rainbow.

if only
it was possible
to heal
as fast as we break

— what if

when you returned
the love i gave you
i thanked you.
it was simply sent to
the wrong address.

— on to the next

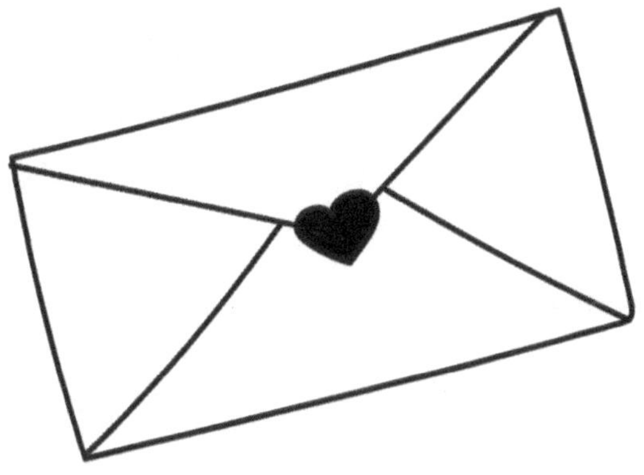

your face.
may be beautiful.
but there is no better way
to impress me.
than the words
leaving it.

they say
you can see the light
in your lover's eyes
but when i look at you
i don't see them there
i see them in your soul.

— the light

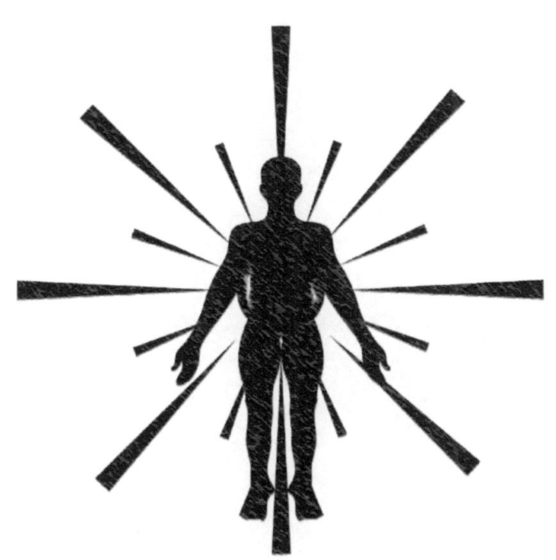

there was the world
with everyone else
and suddenly my world
became you.

— how the universe came to be

reginald stowe

there is so much
honesty in
the way the
midnight sky
gives me room
to breathe.

— night owl

sunsets in harlem

tonight was the first night
my heart wandered back to you
and i have gone
twenty-three painless days without him
a mixture of closure
in the palm of my hands
painting itself onto the canvas
as my life falls into place

— sober

your hands on my body
makes me feel like
your greatest masterpiece.

sitting next to you
with sunshine between
my teeth.
your lips reaching for mine.
i tasted love on my tounge
for the first time.
and it was far sweeter than i
expected it to be.
the moonlight
swallowed us that
hazy summer night.
and i fell in love.
slipping sweetly
into a dream
i never wanted to end.

— june 26

when a boy.
tells you
he loves you.
he means
you must prepare
to travel
the hottest of deserts.
the coldest of nights.
to please him.
when a man tells you
he loves you.
he will take you
far more places
before you have
even left the bed.

— boy vs. man

they say lightning never strikes
in the same place twice.
however
if they only knew
what your love felt like
when i laid eyes upon you
for the first time.

live in this moment with me
so i can forget what life was like
before i met you and
not even think of what life could be
without you.

— simple moments

my dear
i will remember
the moments
you have made me
feel most loved
more than all the times
you have said
i love you.

just because
they do not understand it
does not mean you are wrong.
or out of place.
you do not owe them an apology
you do not owe them your grace.
do not let new age colonialism
or their incapability to
understand language
take away even more from
what has been taken from you.

— 'ghetto'

the sun and moon
may never see each other
but their light
still shines in both.

— long distance friendships

7 billion hearts
and the only one
i want is yours.

— no one else

sunsets in harlem

i am not a kink
or your favorite pornography.
i came from the womb
just like you.
where my mother gave up
her dreams
in order for mine to be.
i am not saying yours
are any less.
but when you only
want me for
your late nights.
or sexual intimacy.
i will refuse.
there is much more to me.
there is so much more
my mother wanted to be.
and to give in to another man's desire
would be a disservice.
to the one who gifted life to me.

the words i write
are not supposed to teach you
how to love me.
they are supposed to teach me
how to love
myself.

— poet

sunsets in harlem

it doesn't have to be over
just come to me a little bit closer
move on for the moment
because i need you more than ever.
bathe me in your indigo sun
and bright cool wind.
oversized shirts
and dances around the kitchen.
look at me in ways
as if you intend to stay
wrap yourself in my arms
until there's no words left to say.
please.
leave your worries at the end of bed
and spill the thoughts inside your head.

— i am home

i know my eyes are not
the colors of the ocean
or the iridescent green of this earth
but these brown eyes
still have hidden mysteries.
secrets of the galaxy.
the ability to become golden honey.
so if you take a moment
look.
and you too can get lost in them
just as much as the others.

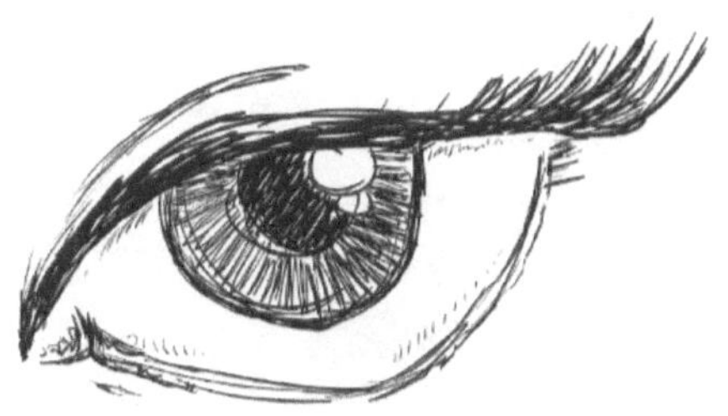

i cannot spend my
whole life
knowing you
as a what if.

— letting go

reginald stowe

i long to be the tears of your eyes

i just hope one day
you'll reach out to me
and i hope that someday
i stop hoping for that.

— hope

reginald stowe

when you ask me
why i write.
i write
to exist.
to be seen.
to hold up a microphone.
for those who look like me.
feel like me.
cry like me.
hurt like me.
because in a world that
refuses to honor my existence.
people like me
deserve to never feel alone.

— i write for you

i was not the greatest at talking
but i was surely the greatest at loving

if my words aren't enough
i said
look into my eyes
and they will tell you the rest.

— honesty

please.
come to me
the moment you feel
homeless.

reginald stowe

sunsets in harlem

what

changed

me.

sunsets in harlem

reginald stowe

the day winter left
i ran home.
mountains fell to their feet.
flowers had risen from the ground
birds began to sing songs of praise.
and the sun had calmed her light.
just for a moment.
it was first time they had seen not seen me
weeping since you left.
who is the boy
they insisted to know
who is the man behind all this happiness
my eyes twinkle
as they all gathered closely to hear
it is me
i have fallen in love
with myself.

i buried past versions of myself
in the ground
and flowers grew from them.
i cradle them like a grieving
child.
combing through their petals
as i pick them off
one by one.
before i bury them too.

— stay in the past

reginald stowe

i needed no better sign
than the world feeling
like it's coming
to an ending
and not hearing
a single word
from you.

— answers

you.
are a perfect sculpture.
of a million dreams.
and memories.
when you doubt your
beauty.
you are breaking the hearts
of your ancestors.
remember.
there is an entire universe.
inside you.

reginald stowe

i have hidden many memories about you
between the lines of my words
i simply close my eyes
and think of the past
as if you're still here
because it is all i have left
to my withered heart
this will not be an easy journey
there will be days where you will feel everything
at once.
the loneliness & grief.
but there will be days where you will be able to
rise again
and move on from everything that was then
i know it will be hard
but better days will come.

— trust me

be kind.
fixing someone
else's wings
will not take
away your ability
to fly.

— kindness is free

reginald stowe

some things
only come into our lives
to helps us grow
when they go.
and sometimes those things.
are people.

when people
tell you that
you are too much
laugh.
because in the end
your cup will be the one
to overflow
fill them up.
for they do not realize
they are empty.

— full

reginald stowe

and when they say
the storm is too strong
i smile and say
so am i.

— the storm

you aren't like anyone i've ever met.
you are right
i wasn't always like this
i learned to bloom
amidst the toughest situations
and when i did
i bloomed fearlessly.
and accepted
i didn't need any other person
to tend to my garden but
myself.

reginald stowe

on the days
when i am not the strongest
i look in the mirror
and admire the color of my skin
and remember the ancestors
that came before me
i thank god that they were able
to stand strong
because generations down the line
their blood
is my blood.
their bravery.
is my backbone.
their dreams
are my destiny to fulfill.
i come from a line of determination.

— honor

i am more
bird than human.
for even the earth.
miles beneath my wings.
cannot call me
home to her.

— wanderlust

they tell me
i am a threat
because my strong personality
vibrant color
firm voice
and determined soul
are considered
too loud
to be tamed
but too much
to be forgotten.

— an unapologetic wildflower

i am sorry
to myself
for not being
the person i needed to be
because you did not see
what you wanted in me.

— an apology

to get lost within myself
not to myself
that is self-love.

isn't it funny
how i am made
from all things
this world
refuses to accept.

— me

this is my wish
for those i love.
to remember me
as a star.
always there
when it gets dark.

— family

not even the stars
beg the world
to see their light.
neither should you.

— confidence

we do not scold flowers
for slow growth.
why must we
rush ourselves.
growth.
is still growth.
no matter the speed of progress.

— the art of growing

the sun kissed my skin
and said
show them what the light can do.

—— melanin

i see things
a little differently
now that
i have
found comfort in
my loneliness.

— mindset

i will no longer allow my body
to be a lighthouse
for those seeking desperation
that ship sailed a long time ago.

— sailor

your ideation of me
is not
my responsibility.

— critics

i still
think of you
as home
even though
someone else
has moved in.

— moving day

for years i climbed
but could never
reach the peak of your expectations
but i made it
not from your failure to realize
but of the painful journey it took
to accept the truth and let that shit go.

— new peaks

i am losing
the connection
to religion based hatred
god fearing bigotry
and accepting
the spirituality
of humanity

— agnostic

every word
is a goodbye.
to a version of myself
that died between the lines.

— it is more than words on paper

i challenge you.
to strip away your outer layers
be vulnerable.
and understand
that your physical attributes
which are beautiful beyond belief
are no match
for holiness and inexhaustible
power of your soul.

— beneath the surface

reginald stowe

i have skin
the color of soil
of course i am meant
to outgrow
people.
places.
you.

— brown skin child

you asked to see me naked.
so i pulled out my pen.
showed you my notebook.
and every poem that bared my soul.
i have stripped myself with these words
and clothed myself stronger.

reginald stowe

sunsets in harlem

182

twenty-one.

sunsets in harlem

reginald stowe

at sixteen the only place i called
home was the bedroom of my own.
where my pillows were only filled with dreams
never centered around another being.

at seventeen the only demons
i fought were the ones in video games.

at eighteen i spent nights
getting drunk on conversations
and saw blue as a color and never a feeling.

at nineteen i had my first love. but i gave myself
to people who gave nothing back. i started to
see every part of myself that lacked.

at twenty i stopped flinching before i got hurt.
and believed that it was a result of errors on
my part.

and twenty-one i did not expect myself to be here.
i figured by now, i'd be six feet deep in soil
pushing up wilted flowers, but i am still here. *i
am still here.* and that is a sign within itself.

at twenty-one i am feeling the light of the sun
and not letting it burn me. at twenty-one i can
feel touch without feeling fear.
and who knew at twenty-one that i can swim an
entire sea of thoughts without drowning?

to my past, thank you for teaching me and to
my present, thank you for sticking around.

i make myself feel better
by saying
you were the wrong person
at the right time
sometimes
i just need a little reminder
of why i am
who i am
without you.
i treat myself so much kinder now.

— reminders

today i chose to let the sun in
and allow joy
to melt this winter
i call sadness.

— moving on i

reginald stowe

sometimes
sadness
is a consequence
for making the right decision.
take your time.

— moving on ii

there will always be an ending.
to everything. remember that.

— appreciation i

you might know a thing or two about this
or maybe you don't
maybe you don't even remember at all
but that night
my heart was beating to the music of your
touch
bodies dancing with alcohol in our blood
revealing hidden parts of me
because you made love feel easy
your hands
connected
like a constellation into mine
our bodies
intertwined
crafting
an
entire
universe
of us.
god the potential of this love
was so good
you couldn't forget it
so beautiful
i couldn't stand it

it was pure.
fucking.
magic.
and
for the first time in our lives
we allowed vulnerability
to show the pieces we had never seen
from drunk kisses and
sober hearts
to broken people secretly
falling apart
it was a brand new start
and you were the missing piece of me.
if that was a dream.
then i am lucky to have
spent every moment of it
with you.

— the dream

if you feel something
when you have written it.
then you have created poetry.
note.
you.
it is your words.
and they do not
belong to anyone else.

— everyone is a writer

time doesn't heal.
you heal yourself.
and that takes time.

— you are much more capable than you know

reginald stowe

i look to the sun
and smile with it.
i realize.
we have both
defeated the storm before
and will again.

— warrior

may the oceans of this earth
remind us
that things can go
as quickly as they come.

— appreciation ii

there's a million thoughts running through my head right now. but i remember sitting in your car in downtown chelsea, scared to make a move. because i knew our time was coming to an end, something you said you were used to. i wish that i could have left everything behind and started over. with you. but time wasn't on our side. however i promise you, *i promise you*. i will never forget this. i will never forget you.

the way the city lights shined against your skin right before i kissed you.
when you made sure i was safe at the bar and always came back by my side.
eating at that random diner in times square.
when we shared one of your marlboro's even though i never smoke.
or that night on the subway when i laid my head on your shoulder
and you said didn't want this to be over.
i wanted time to stop and just live in that very moment, with you.
what can i say, nj?

sunsets in harlem

you showed me who i deserve.
and when i told you i was leaving tomorrow,
i remember you held me and told me you didn't
want to let go.
now here i am dancing around my bedroom as
if you're still here
reminiscing on every moment hoping you'd
walk through the door.
when i was with you.
i felt like i travelled the world.
and if i am no more a memory. to you.
i hope i am one that makes you smile
with every passing thought.

— an open letter to my nj

reginald stowe

one day.
i will find
the love
i always find
myself
writing about.

i sometimes
visualize that i'm a sweet breeze
that whispers secrets of nothing
to anything that will listen
occasionally making the flowers
blush just a little.

— secret insecurities

there is a love that is waiting for me.
i feel it.
moving softly.
taking every step.
slowly and methodically
across time.
so that when it arrives
i will not wither
from the pain of past.
not even in the slightest chance
will it make these petals fall.

— patience

you will never live
your dreams
until you stop living
your fears.

— let it go

my hope will climb
on summits much higher
than the doubt i stood
upon yesterday.

— optimist

i have given
too many pieces
of myself away
and i am tired.
you can have all of me
or none of me
choose.

reginald stowe

vulnerability
snuck upon me
like a scared child
afraid to sleep
in the dark
any longer.

sunsets in harlem

i used to think my independence
was a curse
or wrong
but i've accepted
i am just not meant for
easily influenced
or gentle hearts.

— independent

reginald stowe

what's the point
of trying to live up to
everyone's expectations
when i can luxuriate in the presence
of myself
and dance in the peace
of knowing that i am free.

— singlehood

you're different, he says. because i crave the unordinary, the odd things, places and secrets only i know about. i can tell you, i forgot what home is from traveling so alone, but if i could take back what i did, i wouldn't.

so you're right, i am not like the others. give me warm smiles & one dollar pizza rather than extravagant dinners. give me hikes around the parkway and sunsets in harlem. call me and show up at my door at 2am with wildflowers you picked along your way & your favorite wine. because there's so much life in this world worth living that all i need is you. your heart and soul. nothing else.

i have learned
to speak gently
to my body.
i have learned that love
is not measured in
what i have lost.
but in the peace
that i have
gained.

— lessons

sunsets in harlem

losing you hurt more than anything
i have ever experienced in my twenty-one
years on earth.
and i have lost a lot of things.
but i know some things are not meant and
love and loss are just an
essential part to this life whether
we like it or not.
life will give.
and it will take.
but it's what we become of it
that makes it so damn powerful.

so if i do have a
soulmate out there.
than i know to my core
that i have met.
and loved one of mine that
even writing about you
just makes me realize everything
i would give for one last
sunset in harlem
with you.

and despite everything i have lost.
i will always be thankful to love
and have been loved like that.

— the book

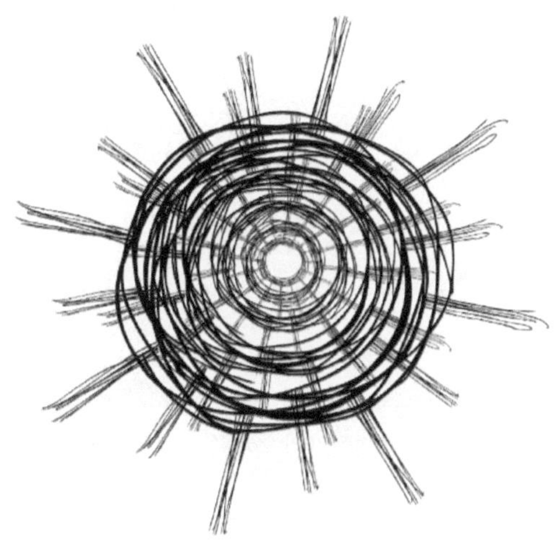

sunsets in harlem

many months ago i couldn't put into words exactly how i felt. i believed my words were meaningless and what i said didn't satisfy the world. and then i asked myself, why do i exist? why do i keep writing? as i stared at these empty pages waiting to be stained, i imagined them connecting to people out here who don't know who they are or where they are going. but remember, you are a living reminder, a soul of purpose. and as an author, i just unravel your wonders and form the alphabet into something magnificent. you are the meaning behind these beautiful words.

perhaps, in my poetry, i've found my courage. and every one of you is the reason why i write, and i can only hope to change someone out there who is a soul just wanting to be happy.

— this is only the beginning

sunsets in harlem

reginald stowe is a city-raised and mountain loving author from charlotte, north carolina. currently getting his bachelor's degree at western carolina university. you can always find him in a book, listening to music, and drinking iced coffee.

poetry is a love that reginald did not discover until these years. as a child, he always found himself reading and writing, but never acknowledged it enough to publish it and perform his work publicly. what used to be something that was only a secret is now a part of him that will never die. there is still so much of him he has to discover and many experiences that are yet to be lived. every day he is figuring out what it means to be human. and this book is one of many to come.

feel free to contact him:
instagram: @stowepoety_
email: rsdawkins1@gmail.com
website: www.reginaldstowepoetry.weebly.com